THE LITTLE RED BOOK OF
YOGA WISDOM

Edited by

KELSIE BESAW

Skyhorse Publishing books may be purchased in bulk at special discounts for sales promotion, corporate gifts, fund-raising, or educational purposes. Special editions can also be created to specifications. For details, contact the Special Sales Department, Skyhorse Publishing, 307 West 36th Street, 11th Floor, New York, NY 10018 or info@skyhorsepublishing.com.

Skyhorse® and Skyhorse Publishing® are registered trademarks of Skyhorse Publishing, Inc.®, a Delaware corporation.

Visit our website at www.skyhorsepublishing.com.

10 9 8 7 6 5 4 3 2 1

Library of Congress Cataloging-in-Publication Data is available on file.

ISBN: 978-1-62636-409-7

Printed in China

CONTENTS

INTRODUCTION

A History

A precise history of yoga is difficult to pin down. Developed over many millennia, the actual term "yoga" wasn't seen until its use in the *Katha Upanishad*, while precursors to the practice of yoga can be seen in multiple ancient sites and texts. The earliest known instance is in seals found at the archeological site of the Indus Valley Civilization, found in modern-day Pakistan and parts of India, Iran, and Afghanistan. These ancient seals, dating to the third millennium BCE, depict poses similar to modern meditation poses, both sitting and standing. While the practices from the Indus Valley Civilization might not have directly influenced later developments that lead to modern yoga, it is certainly illuminating to see the similarities in the disciplines of practitioners that lived thousands of years ago to those of today.

The earliest known texts with references to an early practice similar to yoga are the four Vedas: *Rig Veda, Sama Veda, Yajur Veda*, and *Atharva Veda*. The oldest of the four, *Rig Veda*, is thought to have been first composed in 1500 BCE, coded in 600 BCE, and first written down in 300 BCE. Within the Vedas are ascetic practices and concentration and bodily postures used by the Vedic priests, which resemble what later developed into the practice of yoga. According to Robert H. Schneider and Jeremy Z. Fields in their book *Total Heart Health: How to Prevent and Reverse Heart*

Disease with the Maharishi Vedic Approach to Health, "Yoga asanas were first prescribed by the ancient Vedic texts thousands of years ago and are said to directly enliven the body's inner intelligence" (page 170).

A continuation of the Vedas and also known as the *Vedanta* ("the end of the Veda"), the Upanishads also included similarities to modern yoga. In fact, the term "yoga" first appears in the *Katha Upanishad*, which dates to around 400 BCE. It describes yoga as the steady control of the senses combined with the cessation of mental activity to reach the supreme state. The Upanishads are a collection of philosophical texts and are at the root of the Hindu religion. There are over 200 recognized Upanishads, the earliest of which is *Brihadaranyaka Upanishad*, dating to 900 BCE and containing an early reference to meditation.

The Bhagavad Gita, a 700-verse scripture that is a part of the Hindu epic *Mahabharata*, dating to between the fifth and second centuries BCE, contains numerous references to yoga. The entire sixth chapter is dedicated to traditional yoga and meditation practice, and three other forms of yoga are introduced: Karma yoga, which is the yoga of action; Bhakti yoga, which is the yoga of devotion; and Jnana yoga, which is the yoga of knowledge. Also contained in the *Mahabharata* is the Mokshadharma section in the twelfth chapter, dated between 300 and 200 BCE. The Mokshadharma details an early form of yoga called *nirodha-yoga*, or the yoga of cessation.

Entering into the last century BCE, we see the development of comprehensive and systematic yoga disciplines. Between 200 BCE and 500 CE, philosophical schools of Buddhism, Jainism, and Hinduism developed and gained disciples, and yoga disciplines from each school took on a solid structure. The oldest surviving texts from this era are the early Buddhist Pali suttas, which date c. 29–17 BCE and give details and instructions on meditative practices and states. The Buddha's ideas about the goal of yoga departed from early beliefs that yoga was a complete cessation of thought; he rather believed that some sort of activity in the mind needed to take place in order to achieve liberation, freedom, from thought.

The Yoga Sutras of Patanjali, commonly attributed to Patanjali, are 196 Indian aphorisms that make up the foundation of the discipline of Raja yoga. There is disagreement between scholars as to their exact date, but it is agreed that they appeared or were compiled between the period of the Maurya Empire (322–185 BCE) and 500 CE. Based on the teachings of Samkhya philosophy, which was formed in the first century CE and is the oldest of Indian schools to reach a coherent form, *The Yoga Sutras of Patanjali* are sometimes referred to as *Patanjala Samkhya*, due to the fact that they coincide dramatically with the teachings of Samkhya philosophy. *The Yoga Sutras* detail the eight limbs, or steps, of Ashtanga yoga: Yama (the five "abstensions"); Niyama (the five "observances"); Asana ("seat," meaning the position used for meditation); Pranayama ("suspending breath"); Pratyahara ("abstraction"); Dharana ("concentration"); Dhyana ("meditation"); and Samadhi ("liberation"). The practice and perfection of the first seven limbs creates the ability to achieve Samadhi, which then can be used to navigate through the various layers of consciousness toward the very center of consciousness.

The *Yoga Yajnavalkya*, dated between the second century BCE and the fourth century CE, was influential towards a number of yoga texts that followed it, including *Hatha Yoga Pradipika*, *Yoga Kundalini*, and the *Yoga Tattva Upanishads*. The *Yoga Yajnavalkya* defined yoga as the union between the individual self and the divine.

Jainism was also quickly developing in the early history of yoga. *Tattvarthasutra*, from the second century CE, defined yoga as the combination and sum of all of the activities of mind, body, and speech.

Fast-forwarding through the early centuries of the Common Era, we come to the Middle Ages, which saw the development of a number of types of yoga and meditation practices, including Hatha yoga, the Bhakti movement, Vajrayana, and Sikhism. The mid-nineteenth century showed a development of interest in yoga practices by Western civilizations. N. C. Paul published *A Treatise on the Yoga Philosophy* in 1851, and Swami Vivekananda toured Europe and the United States in the 1890s in order to actively bolster and circulate the aspects of yoga and yoga philosophy.

Today, yoga in the West is thought of mainly in its links with asanas (poses) and as a form of exercise. Many yoga experts have come from the East to promote and spread the yoga philosophy throughout the modern era, namely B. K. S. Iyengar, Swami Satchidananda, and Sri Krishna Pattabhi Jois, among many others.

The Wisdom in this Book

In the following chapters, you will find wisdom from a multitude of authors, from both antiquity and modernity. Many of these are well-known phrases and bits of advice that have circulated among the community; others will be completely new to you. Dispersed throughout the insightful quotes are a list of styles of yoga and yoga poses that are meant to help you find what works best for you.

The quotes have been divided by the wisdom they provide, so that every chapter contains quotes pertaining to its value. Numerous yogis and teachers and practitioners have attempted to define what yoga is or isn't, which has inevitably led to the numerous forms of yoga that are available. The first chapter is a testimony to these many forms of yoga.

With the move from yoga as a state of mind and yoga as a practice for the body, there are numerous tidbits of wisdom pertaining to the mind or the body. You can use these chapters to take wisdom from both sets of voices to help your practice both mentally and physically.

Gautama Buddha is one of the most well-known voices in the history of yoga and Buddhist philosophy. His wisdom can be gleaned from everything involving yoga, inspiration, life, and death. His quotes on enlightenment and his quotes on love truly show him for the guru he was.

We narrow the focus with some quotes that particularly denote the practice of traditional hot yoga and Bikram yoga. These quotes are effortless in their inspiration and will help you get through those grueling ninety minutes of intense heat and focus.

Buddha wasn't the only great mind of yoga, so I have gathered a sweeping collection of quotes that include authors of a variety of time periods and practices. Included are ancient minds such as Patanjali and Gandhi as well as more modern minds such as Sting and Jennifer Aniston. The words in this chapter will inspire you no matter what type of yoga you do and no matter where you come from.

As breathing is one of the most important aspects of yoga and meditation, I have included a chapter dedicated to that wonderful action of filling your lungs and exhaling all that you do not need. Inhale deeply through this thought-provoking section, and exhale your way into enlightenment, which, coincidentally (wink wink), is what the following chapter is dedicated to.

Yoga is a serious activity and can be intense and draining on both your mind and your body. But yoga is not all breathing and pushing your body to the limits. Smiling, laughing, and being happy in your practice are also important aspects of yoga. This chapter is meant to make you smile, laugh, and nod your head along with those who have made the same silly mistakes and oops.

Focusing on poses is the next chapter of this book, where you will read what others feel and think in certain poses. While everyone experiences yoga differently, this section is a nice tribute to all things asana and what everyone experiences during their own bodys' movements. We proceed into the journey of yoga, which is a particularly important thing to grasp during the practice of yoga. Very rarely does something click without having to do any work. Taking the journey of yoga, both mentally and physically, means just that: going on a journey.

We conclude this book of quotes where you would conclude any yoga class: meditation. Meditation has been involved in yoga for thousands of years and even seems to be what yoga developed from. Meditation is crucial in achieving enlightenment, and it is essential in the practice of yoga. These quotes will help you focus your mind and delve into the deepest recesses of your Self.

Happy journeying!
Kelsie Besaw
New York City

1

WHAT IS YOGA?

Yoga teaches us to cure what need not be endured and endure what cannot be cured.
—B. K. S. Iyengar

• • •

To perform every action artfully is yoga.
—Swami Kripalu

• • •

You cannot do yoga. Yoga is your natural state. What you can do are yoga exercises, which may reveal to you where you are resisting your natural state.
—SHARON GANNON

• • •

Yoga is 99% practice and 1% theory.
—SRI KRISHNA PATTABHI JOIS

• • •

Yoga is the practice of quieting the mind.
—PATANJALI

• • •

Yoga is a way to freedom. By its constant practice, we can free ourselves from fear, anguish, and loneliness.
—INDRA DEVI

• • •

Yoga is skillful action.
—*THE BHAGAVAD GITA*

• • •

What Is Yoga?

Yoga is almost like music in a way; there's no end to it.
—STING

• • •

Yoga aims to remove the root cause of all diseases, not to treat its
symptoms as medical science generally attempts to do.
—SWAMI VISHNU-DEVANANDA

• • •

Yoga is about compassion and generosity toward others. It means
being mindful of the world around us.
—CHRISTY TURLINGTON

• • •

Yoga carves you into a different person—and that is
satisfying physically.
—ADAM LEVINE

• • •

Yoga is an art and science of living. Yoga means union, in all its
significances and dimensions.
—INDRA DEVI

• • •

The man who sees me in everything
and everything within me
will not be lost to me, nor
will I ever be lost to him.

He who is rooted in oneness
realizes that I am
in every being; wherever
he goes, he remains in me.

When he sees all being as equal
in suffering or in joy
because they are like himself,
that man has grown perfect in yoga.
—*The Bhagavad Gita*

● ● ●

Yoga calms me down. It's a therapy session, a workout, and meditation all at the same time!
—*Jennifer Aniston*

● ● ●

Exercises are like prose, whereas yoga is the poetry of movements. Once you understand the grammar of yoga; you can write your poetry of movements.
—AMIT RAY, *YOGA AND VIPASSANA: AN INTEGRATED LIFE STYLE*

• • •

Yoga is about remembering that we are already one with the divinity and we've never left it.
—GUY DONAHAYE AND EDDIE STERN, *GURUJI: A PORTRAIT OF SRI K. PATTABHI JOIS THROUGH THE EYES OF HIS STUDENTS*

• • •

A mind free from all disturbance is Yoga.
—PATANJALI,
THE YOGA SUTRAS OF PATANJALI

• • •

For me, yoga is not just a workout—it's about working on yourself.
—MARY GLOVER

• • •

Yoga is a young child playing.
—SADGURU SHREE SHREE ALLOWAH-GEE MAHARAJ

• • •

All life is a secret Yoga, an obscure growth of Nature towards the discovery and fulfilment of the divine principle hidden in her which becomes progressively less obscure, more self-conscient and luminous, more self-possessed in the human being by the opening of all his instruments of knowledge, will, action, life to the Spirit within him and in the world.

—Sri Aurobindo,
The Synthesis of Yoga

• • •

Yoga is the cessation of the movements of the mind. Then there is abiding in the Seer's own form.

—Patanjali,
The Yoga Sutras of Patanjali

• • •

Yoga will always be transformational, even when it stops being cool.

—Victoria Moran,
*Younger by the Day:
365 Ways to Rejuvenate Your Body
and Revitalize Your Spirit*

• • •

Arjuna said: Those devotees who thus by a constant union seek after Thee, and those who seek after the unmanifest Immutable, which of these have the greater knowledge of Yoga?
—*THE BHAGAVAD GITA*

• • •

Yoga is the martial art of the soul, and the opponent is the strongest you've ever faced: your ego.
—UNKNOWN

• • •

Kundalini yoga is a comprehensive path of growth and life that demands neither asceticism nor seclusion. It is much more about linking together the spiritual practice and the everyday life of those who practice it.
—ATHANASIOS KARTA SINGH, *KUNDALINI YOGA: TECHNIQUES FOR DEVELOPING STRENGTH, AWARENESS, AND CHARACTER*

• • •

Whatever you do in life, yoga shows you how to do it better.
—CHUCK MILLER

• • •

Yoga is invigoration in relaxation. Freedom in routine. Confidence through self control. Energy within and energy without.
—YMBER DELECTO

• • •

The principle of Yoga is the turning of one or of all powers of our human existence into a means of reaching divine Being.
—SRI AUROBINDO,
THE SYNTHESIS OF YOGA

• • •

Self-healing is the privilege of every person. Self-healing is not a miracle and has nothing to do with doing something, being able to do something. Self-healing is a process that develops from the relationship of the body with the infinite power of the soul. It is an engagement, a unity—that is the science of Kundalini Yoga.
—YOGI BHAJAN

• • •

Yoga exists in the world because everything is linked.
—DESIKASHAR

• • •

Yoga science is not just a scholarly pursuit. It is a moment by moment and thought by thought practical guide for living.
—LEONARD PERLMUTTER,
THE HEART AND SCIENCE OF YOGA

• • •

Yoga is not a religion. It is a science, science of well-being, science of youthfulness, science of integrating body, mind and soul.
—AMIT RAY, *YOGA AND VIPASSANA:
AN INTEGRATED LIFE STYLE*

• • •

When you listen to yourself, everything comes naturally. It comes from inside, like a kind of will to do something. Try to be sensitive. That is yoga.
— PETRI RÄISÄNEN

• • •

What is yoga? The essence of yoga is to withdraw the mind from all external activities, draw it inward, and keep it contained within [*laya*]. The example of sleep is a way to illustrate the benefits of yoga. However, the withdrawal of the mind from external activities during sleep is due to the influence of *tamas* [the quality of dullness that clouds the mind]. The inward turning or steadiness of the mind in yoga is due to *sattva* [the quality of clarity and knowing in the mind]. The steadiness of mind brought about by *sattva* is a thousand times more beneficial than that brought about by *tamas*, though it may not be common knowledge to all. This [steadiness of the mind due to *sattva*] is *yoga-nidra*. In fact, all of our time is wasted until we attain such steadiness of mind through yoga.

—SRI TIRUMALAI KRISHNAMACHARYA,
YOGA MAKARANDA

• • •

Practicing yoga during the day is a matter of keeping your eyes on the road and one ear turned toward the infinite. It's about listening inwardly as often as you can for your deepest impulses about what to say, think, do, or be.

—ERICH SCHIFFMANN, *YOGA: THE SPIRIT AND PRACTICE OF MOVING INTO STILLNESS*

• • •

Yoga, an ancient but perfect science, deals with the evolution of
humanity. This evolution includes all aspects of one's being, from
bodily health to self-realization. Yoga means union—
the union of body with consciousness and consciousness
with the soul.
—B. K. S. IYENGAR

• • •

Yoga does not remove us from the reality or responsibilities of
everyday life but rather places our feet firmly and resolutely in
the practical ground of experience. We don't transcend our lives;
we return to the life we left behind in the hopes of
something better.
—DONNA FARHI, *BRINGING YOGA TO LIFE*

• • •

The attitude of gratitude is the highest yoga.
—YOGI BHAJAN

• • •

Yoga is possible for anybody who really wants it. Yoga is universal. . . . But don't approach yoga with a business mind looking for worldly gain.
—SRI KRISHNA PATTABHI JOIS

• • •

Let your practice be a celebration of life.
—SEIDO LEE DEBARROS

• • •

Yoga is not gymnastics or a competition. The goal is not to achieve an outwardly perfect form through excessive ambition but rather to experience your own spirituality and the interaction of body and mind in each pose.
—ATHANASIOS KARTA SINGH,
KUNDALINI YOGA:
TECHNIQUES FOR DEVELOPING STRENGTH,
AWARENESS, AND CHARACTER

• • •

Crying is one of the highest devotional songs. One who knows crying, knows spiritual practice. If you can cry with a pure heart, nothing else compares to such a prayer. Crying includes all the principles of Yoga.
—SWAMI KRIPALU

• • •

Yoga is about awakening. Yoga is about creating a life that brings more beauty and more love into the world.
—JOHN FRIEND

• • •

When this body has been so magnificently and artistically created by God, it is only fitting that we should maintain it in good health and harmony by the most excellent and artistic science of Yoga.
—GEETA IYENGAR, *YOGA: A GEM FOR WOMEN*

• • •

The real Meaning of Yoga is a deliverance from contact with pain and sorrow.
—*THE BHAGAVAD GITA*

• • •

Vogue and *Self* are putting out the message of yoginis as buff and perfect. If you start doing yoga for those reasons, fine. Most people get beyond that and see that it's much, much more.
—PATRICIA WALDEN

• • •

The Yoga of action, leading to union with the soul is fiery aspiration, spiritual reading and devotion to Ishvara.
—PATANJALI, *THE YOGA SUTRAS OF PATANJALI*

• • •

Spiritual practices help us move from identifying with the ego to identifying with the soul.
—RAM DASS

• • •

Yoga is the unifying art of transforming dharma into action, be it through inspired thought, properly nurturing our children, a painting, a kindness or an act of peace that forever moves humanity forward.
—MICHELINE BERRY

• • •

Yoga doesn't ask you to be more than you are. But it does ask you to be all that you are.
—BRYAN KEST

• • •

Just as all rivers end up in the ocean, all forms of Yoga end up raising the Kundalini. Kundalini is the creative potential of every human being.
—YOGI BHAJAN

• • •

Kriya Yoga consists of body discipline, mental control, and meditating on *Aum*.
—PATANJALI,
THE YOGA SUTRAS OF PATANJALI

• • •

He who has no egoism, no I-ness and my-ness, who has friendship and pity for all beings and hate for no living thing, who
has a tranquil equality to pleasure and pain, and is patient and
forgiving, he who has a desireless content, the steadfast control of
self and the firm unshakable will and resolution of the Yogin and
a love and devotion which gives up the whole mind and reason to
Me, he is dear to Me.
—*The Bhagavad Gita*

• • •

The quality of your practice is ultimately measured by its effect
on the quality of your life. In other words, mastery in yoga is
mastery of life.
—Rod Stryker,
"Upward-Facing Bow,"
www.parayoga.com

• • •

2

STYLES OF YOGA

There are many different yoga practices. This list should help you choose which one is best for you.

Ananda: Classes that practice this style of yoga focus on proper body alignment, controlled breathing, and gentle postures that are designed to move the energy toward the brain.

Anusara: This style focuses on heart-opening poses such as backbends.

Astanga: Also known as Power Yoga, this is a style that will push your body to the limit.

Bikram: With a set room temperature of between 95 degress and 105 degress Fahrenheit, this type of yoga helps promote flexibility and induces cleansing through sweat. This class is great for beginners because of its set twenty-six postures and focus on alignment.

Hatha: In this style of yoga, the focus is on slow, gentle movement.

Jivamukti: Jivamukti mixes vinyasa flow with sequences with chanting and also encourages a vegetarian/vegan lifestyle.

Integral: Founded by Sri Aurobindo in the early 1900s, this style of yoga combines the Physical, Vital, Mental, Psychic, and Spiritual aspects of human beings in order to transform the entire being. This is not to be confused by the Integral Yoga Institute, founded by followers of Sri Swami Satchidananda, which focuses on Hatha yoga practice.

ISHTA: This style of yoga, founded by South African teacher Mani Finger and popularized in the states by his son Alan, utilizes postures, visualizations, and breathing to help open the channels of energy throughout the body.

Iyengar: Here you will get a strong focus on alignment with the use of props such as blocks, straps, harnesses, and cushions.

Kali Ray TriYoga: This style combines pranayama breathing exercises and meditation with flowing dancelike movements.

Kripalu: Combining physical postures, breathing techniques, deep relaxation, and meditation, this style's aim is to remove any blocks that prevent energy from moving through the body.

Kundalini: Expect an intense practice with this style. "Kundalini" refers to the energy of the Root Chakra, which surrounds the low spine, and classes tend to focus on the core area.

Prenatal: This style tends to focus on breathing and core work and is said to be the best style of yoga for pregnant women.

Restorative: Focusing on relaxation, this is the best style of yoga to help you wind down at the end of the day.

Sivananda: Similar to Integral Yoga, this practice combines breathing, meditation, chanting, dietary restrictions, scriptural study, and postures in an aim to preserve the health and wellness of the practitioner.

Svaroopa®: A style that is available to all people of all ages and levels, Svaroopa focuses on the muscles surrounding the spine.

Viniyoga™: This is a style that is designed to bend to the will of the practitioner and his or her own specific needs.

Vinyasa: This style of yoga, also called vinyasa flow or flow, is exactly how it sounds: flowing from pose to pose. Except for the initial sun salutations, no vinyasa practice is ever the same.

Yin: This style of yoga is meant to counter yang forms of yoga (Ashtanga, Hatha, Iyengar, etc.). It focuses on lengthy poses that can last from five to twenty minutes, promoting flexibility, patience, and the ability to quiet the mind.

3

YOGA AND THE BODY

You are as young as your spine is flexible.
—Ancient yogic adage

• • •

The foot feels the foot when it feels the ground.
—Gautama Buddha

• • •

Not only is yoga excellent for flexibility, but it is also a great tool for longevity and injury prevention, as it allows for internal body awareness.
—KYLE SHEWFELT

• • •

Your body is precious. It is our vehicle for awakening. Treat it with care.
—GAUTAMA BUDDHA

• • •

Take care of your body. It's the only place you have to live.
—JIM ROHN

• • •

The body is your temple. Keep it pure and clean for the soul to reside in.
—B. K. S. IYENGAR

• • •

Fall with awareness and acceptance.
—BRYAN KEST

• • •

Yoga practice can make us more and more sensitive to subtler
and subtler sensations in the body. Paying attention to and
staying with finer and finer sensations within the body is one of
the surest ways to steady the wandering mind.
—RAVI RAVINDRA,
*THE WISDOM OF PATANJALI'S YOGA SUTRAS:
A NEW TRANSLATION AND GUIDE*

• • •

It's bizarre that the produce manager is more important to my
children's health than the pediatrician.
—MERYL STREEP

• • •

Lack of activity destroys the good condition of every human being, while movement and methodical physical exercise save it and preserve it.
—PLATO

• • •

Yoga is essentially a practice for your soul, working through the medium of your body.
—TARA FRASER

• • •

Symmetry of form, beauty of color, strength and the compactness of the diamond, constitute bodily perfection.
—PATANJALI,
THE YOGA SUTRAS OF PATANJALI

• • •

For someone like me, who loves to sweat and push herself, it's a
challenge to slow down, to sit, to breathe and hold poses.
—Ellen DeGeneres

• • •

Welcome to your body.
—Bryan Kest

• • •

The first thing that you must learn to understand as a human
being is the instrument of your movement—the physical body.
All these systems (glandular system, circulatory system, respira-
tory sytem, heartbeat, brain, and nervous system) are connected
with one another via a structure of flesh and bones. It is a func-
tionally cohesive system. And as such, it needs attention, care,
and fine-tuning.
—Yogi Bhajan

• • •

Basketball is an endurance sport, and you have to learn to control your breath; that's the essence of yoga, too. So, I consciously began using yoga techniques in my practice and playing. I think yoga helped reduce the number and severity of injuries I suffered. As preventative medicine, it's unequaled.
—KAREEM ABDUL-JABBAR

• • •

4

YOGA AND THE MIND

The sequence of mental states is as follows: the mind reacts to that which is seen; then follows the moment of mind control. Then ensues a moment wherein the chitta (mind stuff) responds to both these factors. Finally these pass away, and the perceiving consciousness has full sway.

—PATANJALI,
THE YOGA SUTRAS OF PATANJALI

• • •

The most important pieces of equipment you need for doing yoga are your mind and your body.
—RODNEY YEE, *YOGA: THE POETRY OF THE BODY*

• • •

Ordinarily the mind is scattered, one portion here, another portion there. It is necessary to collect the scattered mind and direct it toward one point.
—RAMAKRISHNA, *THE GOSPEL OF RAMAKRISHNA*, EDITED BY SWAMI ABHEDANANDA

• • •

Meditate. Live purely. Quiet the mind. Do your work with mastery. Like the moon, come out from behind the clouds! Shine.
—GAUTAMA BUDDHA

• • •

You must transform and transcend your unconscious habit of pitying yourself and having feelings of inferiority if you want to grow and feel the experience of your mind reaching into infinity.
—YOGI BHAJAN

• • •

Mindfulness helps you go home to the present. And every time you go there and recognize a condition of happiness that you have, happiness comes.
—THICH NHAT HANH

• • •

The cause of *bandha* and *moksha* (bondage and liberation) is our own minds. If we think we are bound, we are bound. If we think we are liberated, we are liberated. . . . It is only when we transcend the mind that we are free from all these troubles.
—PATANJALI,
THE YOGA SUTRAS OF PATANJALI

• • •

All I'm saying is that to liberate the potential of your mind, body and soul, you must first expand your imagination. You see, things are always created twice: first in the workshop of the mind and then, and only then, in reality. I call this process 'blueprinting' because anything you create in your outer world began as a simple blueprint in your inner world.
—ROBIN SHARMA,
THE MONK WHO SOLD HIS FERRARI

• • •

The beauty is that people often come here for the stretch, and leave with a lot more.
—LIZA CIANO

• • •

Yoga has a sly, clever way of short circuiting the mental patterns
that cause anxiety.
—BAXTER BELL

• • •

To bring body and mind into a harmonious balance, it is
necessary to open the chakras. Blocked energy hubs, when either
closed or only slightly opened, can bring about physical and
psychic dysfunction or insensitivities.
—ATHANASIOS KARTA SINGH,
KUNDALINI YOGA:
TECHNIQUES FOR DEVELOPING STRENGTH,
AWARENESS, AND CHARACTER

• • •

Undisturbed calmness of mind is attained by cultivating friendliness toward the happy, compassion for the unhappy, delight in the virtuous, and indifference toward the wicked.
—PATANJALI,
THE YOGA SUTRAS OF PATANJALI

• • •

By means of personal experimentation and observation, we can discover certain simple and universal truths. The mind moves the body, and the body follows the mind. Logically then, negative thought patterns harm not only the mind but also the body. What we actually do builds up to affect the subconscious mind and in turn affects the conscious mind and all reactions.
—H. E. DAVEY,
*JAPANESE YOGA:
THE WAY OF DYNAMIC MEDITATION*

• • •

You are a living magnet. What you attract in your life is harmony with your dominant thoughts.
—BRIAN TRACY

• • •

The soul always knows what to do to heal itself. The challenge is
to silence the mind.
—Caroline Myss

• • •

The man who can discriminate between the soul and the spirit
achieves supremacy over all conditions and becomes omniscient.
—Patanjali,
The Yoga Sutras of Patanjali

• • •

When your mind, which has been tossed about by conflicting
opinions, becomes still and centered in equilibrium, then you
experience Yoga.
—*The Bhagavad Gita*

• • •

Thoughts contrary to yoga are harmfulness, falsehood, theft, incontinence, and avarice, whether committed personally, caused to be committed or approved of, whether arising from avarice, anger or delusion (ignorance); whether slight in the doing, middling or great. These result always in excessive pain and ignorance. For this reason, the contrary thoughts must be cultivated.
—PATANJALI,
THE YOGA SUTRAS OF PATANJALI

• • •

When the mind is calm, how quickly, how smoothly, how beautifully you will perceive everything.
—PARAMAHANSA YOGANANDA

• • •

I don't eat junk foods and I don't think junk thoughts.
—PEACE PILGRIM

• • •

Every waking moment we talk to ourselves about the things we experience. Our self-talk, the thoughts we communicate to ourselves, in turn control the way we feel and act.
—JOHN LEMBO

• • •

Body is not stiff, mind is stiff.
—SRI KRISHNA PATTABHI JOIS

• • •

Keep your feet on the ground and your thoughts at lofty heights.
—PEACE PILGRIM

• • •

In the mirror of your mind all kinds of pictures appear and disappear. Knowing that they are entirely your own creations, watch them silently come and go. Be alert, but not perturbed. This attitude of silent observation is the very foundation of yoga. You see the picture, but you are not the picture.
—NISARGADATTA MAHARAJ,
I AM THAT

• • •

If you realized how powerful your thoughts are, you would never
think a negative thought.
—Peace Pilgrim

• • •

Physically, it completely changed me. I found strength that I
never thought I had. And mentally, I mean, it's taught me just
patience and letting go, and it's really changed my whole psychological outlook, I think.
—Gwyneth Paltrow

• • •

5

GAUTAMA BUDDHA

The mind is everything. What you think, you become.

• • •

To force oneself to believe and to accept a thing without understanding is political, and not spiritual or intellectual.

• • •

You will not be punished for your anger, you will be punished by your anger.

• • •

As rain falls equally on the just and the unjust, do not burden your heart with judgments but rain your kindness equally on all.

• • •

If you light a lamp for somebody, it will also brighten your path.

• • •

There is nothing so disobedient as an undisciplined mind, and there is nothing so obedient as a disciplined mind.

• • •

Happiness follows sorrow, sorrow follows happiness, but when one no longer discriminates happiness and sorrow, a good deal and a bad deed, one is able to realize freedom.

• • •

Those who are free of resentful thoughts surely find peace.

• • •

Hatred does not cease by hatred, but only by love; this is the eternal rule.

• • •

As a flower that is lovely and beautiful, but is scentless, even so fruitless is the well-spoken word of one who practices it not.

• • •

If the selflessness of phenomena is analyzed and if this analysis is cultivated, it causes the effect of attaining nirvana. Through no other cause does one come to peace.

• • •

Just as a candle cannot burn without fire, men cannot live without a spiritual life.

• • •

The way is not in the sky. The way is in the heart.

• • •

Most problems, if you give them enough time and space, will eventually wear themselves out.

• • •

Resolve to be tender with the young, compassionate with the aged, sympathetic with the striving, and tolerant with the weak and wrong. Sometime in your life, you will have been all of these.

• • •

Whatever words we utter should be chosen with care, for people will hear them and be influenced by them for good or ill.

• • •

All descriptions of reality are temporary hypotheses.

• • •

I never see what has been done; I only see what remains to be done.

• • •

You only lose what you cling to.

• • •

Our theories of the eternal are as valuable as are those that a chick which has not broken its way through its shell might form of the outside world.

• • •

We are what we think. All that we are arises with our thoughts. With our thoughts, we make the world.

• • •

Just as treasures are uncovered from the earth, so virtue appears from good deeds, and wisdom appears from a pure and peaceful mind. To walk safely through the maze of human life, one needs the light of wisdom and the guidance of virtue.

• • •

To be idle is a short road to death and to be diligent is a way of life; foolish people are idle, wise people are diligent.

• • •

He is able who thinks he is able.

• • •

A man is not called wise because he talks and talks again; but if he is peaceful, loving and fearless then he is in truth called wise.

• • •

You can search throughout the entire universe for someone who is more deserving of your love and affection than you are yourself, and that person is not to be found anywhere. You yourself, as much as anybody in the entire universe, deserve your love and affection.

• • •

To keep the body in good health is a duty . . . otherwise we shall not be able to keep our mind strong and clear.

• • •

Wear your ego like a loose fitting garment.

• • •

Let us rise up and be thankful, for if we didn't learn a lot at least we learned a little, and if we didn't learn a little, at least we didn't get sick, and if we got sick, at least we didn't die; so, let us all be thankful.

• • •

Silence the angry man with love. Silence the ill-natured man with kindness. Silence the miser with generosity. Silence the liar with truth.

• • •

The whole secret of existence is to have no fear. Never fear what will become of you, depend on no one. Only the moment you reject all help are you freed.

• • •

If your compassion does not include yourself, it is incomplete.

• • •

Nothing is forever except change.

• • •

The wise ones fashioned speech with their thought, sifting it as grain is sifted through a sieve.

• • •

Health is the greatest prize, contentment is the mightiest wealth. A reliable friend is the best kinsman and Nirvana is the ultimate happiness.

• • •

When the student is ready, the teacher will appear.

• • •

Peace comes from within. Do not seek it without.

• • •

May we live like the lotus, at home in muddy water.

• • •

A man asked Gautama Buddha, "I want happiness." Buddha said, "First remove 'I,' that's Ego, then remove 'want,' that's Desire. See now you are left with only 'Happiness.'"

• • •

There is no path to happiness: happiness is the path.

• • •

I consider the positions of kings and rulers as that of dust motes. I observe treasure of gold and gems as so many bricks and pebbles. I look upon the finest silken robes as tattered rags. I see myriad worlds of the universe as small seeds of fruit, and the greatest lake in India as a drop of oil on my foot. I perceive the teachings of the world to be the illusion of magicians. I discern the highest conception of emancipation as golden brocade in a dream, and view the holy path of the illuminated one as flowers appearing in one's eyes. I see meditation as a pillar of a mountain, Nirvana as a nightmare of daytime. I look upon the judgment of right and wrong as the serpentine dance of a dragon, and the rise and fall of beliefs as but traces left by the four seasons.

• • •

Believe nothing, no matter where you read it, or who said it, no matter if I have said it, unless it agrees with your own reason and common sense.

• • •

Praise and blame, gain and loss, pleasure and sorrow come and go like the wind. To be happy, rest like a giant tree in the midst of them all.

• • •

Holding on to anger is like grasping a hot coal with the intent of throwing it at someone else; you are the one who gets burned.

• • •

Thousands of candles can be lighted from a single candle, and the life of the candle will not be shortened. Happiness never decreases by being shared.

• • •

Opinion, O disciples, is a disease; opinion is a tumor; opinion is a sore. He who has overcome all opinion, O disciples, is called a saint, one who knows.

• • •

Everything that has a beginning has an ending. Make your peace with that and all will be well.

• • •

When you realize how perfect everything is, you will tilt your head back and laugh at the sky.

• • •

Three things cannot be long hidden: the sun, the moon, and the truth.

• • •

Even death is not to be feared by one who has lived wisely.

• • •

Be vigilant; guard your mind against negative thoughts.

• • •

Doubt everything. Find your own light.

• • •

Holding onto anger is like drinking poison and expecting the other person to die.

• • •

6

YOGA POSES

The poses in yoga are countless. Here is a list that will help you determine which poses will benefit your body the most. This list is nowhere near comprehensive but provides basic information about the most common yoga poses.

• • •

Name of the Pose	Name in Sanskrit	What Are the Benefits?
Arm Balance Scorpion	Bhuja Vrischikasana	Strengthens wrists and arms; improves balance, stability, and flexibility; promotes concentration and focus
Balancing Stick	Tuladandasana	Strengthens core and leg muscles and improves stamina
Bharadvaja's Twist	Bharadvajasana I	A restorative for the spine and abdominal organs
Big Toe Pose	Padangusthasana	Lengthens and stretches hamstrings
Bound Angle Pose	Baddha Konasana	A wonderful groin- and hip-opener
Bow Pose	Dhanurasana	Strengthens all of the muscles along the spine

Name of the Pose	Name in Sanskrit	What Are the Benefits?
Breath Retention	Kumbhaka Pranayama	Strengthens the lungs and brings more oxygen to the bloodstream to aid in deeper breaths
Bridge Pose	Setu Bandha Sarvangasana	Opens the chest and promotes spinal flexibility
Camel Pose	Ustrasana	Opens the heart, stretches the hip flexors and abdominal walls, and increases flexibility in the spine
Cat Pose	Marjaryasana	Gently massages the spine and the abdominal organs
Chair Pose or Awkward Pose	Ustkatasana	Strengthens the muscles of the arms and legs while also stimulating the diaphragm and heart
Channel Cleaning Breath	Nadi Shodhana Pranayama	Lessens anxiety and stress and slows heart rate

Name of the Pose	Name in Sanskrit	What Are the Benefits?
Child's Pose	Balasana	A restorative pose that releases tension in the back, shoulders, and chest and alleviates stress and anxiety
Cobra Pose	Bhujangasana	A heart opener that increases flexibility in the spine and strengthens the muscles surrounding the low spine
Cockerel/ Rooster Pose	Kukkutasana	Strengthens wrists, arms, and shoulders as well as the abdominal muscles
Conqueror Breath	Ujjayi Pranayama	Smoothes and slows the flow of breath, while also quieting the mind
Corpse Pose	Savasana	Total and complete relaxation of every muscle in the body
Cow Face Pose	Gomukhasana	Targets hips and shoulders for increased flexibility and release of tension

Name of the Pose	Name in Sanskrit	What Are the Benefits?
Cow Pose	Bitilasana	A gentle spinal warm-up
Crane Pose	Bakasana	Tones and strengthens abdominal organs and arms
Crocodile Pose	Nakrasana	Gently lengthens the spine, releases lower back tension, and promotes relaxation
Deer Seal	Mrigi Mudra	Helps to control pranayama with a traditional hand seal or gesture
Diamond Pose	Vajrasana	Relieves sciatic pain
Dolphin Plank Pose	—	Useful for strengthening and toning arms, core, and thighs
Dolphin Pose	Makarasana	A shoulder-opener that strengthens core, arms, and legs

Name of the Pose	Name in Sanskrit	What Are the Benefits?
Downward-Facing Dog Pose	Adho Mukha Svanasana	An all-over, re-energizing stretch
Eagle Pose	Garudasana	Promotes, strength, flexibility, and endurance; a deep shoulder-opener
Ear Pressure Pose	Karnapidasana	Opens the shoulders and helps to align the spine
Easy Pose	Sukhasana	Helps to correct spinal alignment
Eight-Angle Pose	Astavakrasana	Tones the abdominal muscles and strengthens the wrists and arms
Extended Hand-to-Big-Toe Pose	Utthita Hasta Padangustasana	Promotes balance and stretches backs of the legs
Extended Puppy Pose	Uttana Shishosana	Lengthens and stretches the spine and promotes relaxation

Name of the Pose	Name in Sanskrit	What Are the Benefits?
Extended Side Angle Pose	Utthita Parsvakonasana	Induces a deep side stretch from the back of the heel through the raised arm; strengthens core and legs
Extended Triangle Pose	Utthita Trikonasana	Helps stretch hips, groins, hamstrings, calves, and spine while opening chest and shoulders
Feathered Peacock Pose, also known as Forearm or Elbow Balance	Pincha Mayurasana	Strengthens arms, back, and shoulders and stretches all of the muscles of the legs, back, stomach, and neck
Fire Log Pose	Agnistambhasana	Promotes an intense stretch in the hips and helps to ease sciatic pain
Firefly Pose	Tittibhasana	Requires maximum abdominal strength and also strengthens the arms

Name of the Pose	Name in Sanskrit	What Are the Benefits?
Fish Pose	Matsyasana	Stretches hip flexors and front body while releasing tension in the throat, neck, and shoulders
Four-Limbed Staff Pose	Chaturanga Dandasana	Strengthens arms and core
Frog Pose	Bhekasana	A deep hip opener that also strengthens the lower back
Full Boat Pose	Paripurna Navasana	Strengthens abdominals and hip flexors
Garland Pose	Malasana	Stretches ankles, spine, and back torso
Gate Pose	Parighasana	Stretches side body, tones the abdominals, improves circulation, and increases flexibility of the spine
Half Frog Pose	Ardha Bhekasana	A backbend that also opens the shoulders, chest, and thighs simultaneously

Name of the Pose	Name in Sanskrit	What Are the Benefits?
Half Locust Pose	Ardha Salabhasana	Improves circulation of blood and strengthens thighs, buttocks, hips, and upper spine muscles
Half Lord of the Fishes Pose, also known as Seated Spinal Twist	Ardha Matsyendrasana	Energizes the spine and stimulates digestive system; this pose is also great at the end of a yoga class, as it helps neutralize the spine
Half Moon Pose	Ardha Chandrasana	Improves balance and strengthens every aspect of the core
Handstand	Adho Mukha Vrksasana	Aids in balance and increases core strength
Happy Baby Pose	Ananda Balasana	Helps bring awareness to the hip joints

Name of the Pose	Name in Sanskrit	What Are the Benefits?
Head-to-Knee Forward Bend	Janu Sirsasana	Helps increase flexibility in the muscles of the backs of the legs and also twists the spine
Hero Pose	Virasana	Stretches the thighs, knees, and ankles and strengthens the arches of the feet
Heron Pose	Krounchasana	Stretches the backs of the legs and strengthens abdominal muscles
High Lunge, sometimes called Horse Rider's Pose	Ashva Sanchalanasana	Strengthens arms and legs and stretches the groin
High Lunge, variation	—	Preparation for the full version of Warrior I Pose

Name of the Pose	Name in Sanskrit	What Are the Benefits?
Intense Side Stretch Pose	Parsvottanasana	Promotes a stretch of the spine, shoulders and wrists, hamstrings, and hips and also strengthens the legs and improves balance
King Pigeon Pose	Kapotasana	An extremely deep backbend that promotes spinal flexibility
Legs-Up-the-Wall Pose	Viparita Karani	A restorative posture that regulates blood flow and has a wide range of health benefits for the body and mind
Lion Pose	Simhasana	Relieves tension in the face and chest
Lizard Pose	Utthan Pristhasana	Opens the thighs and stretches spine, hamstrings, and lower back

Name of the Pose	Name in Sanskrit	What Are the Benefits?
Locust Pose	Salabhasana	Strengthens the mid-spinal muscles as well as the legs and arms
Lord of the Dance Pose	Natarajasana	Stretches the entire body and improves posture and balance
Lotus Pose	Padmasana	Stretches the ankles and knees; stimulates the pelvis, spine, abdomen, and bladder; calms the brain; eases menstrual pain and sciatica
Low Lunge	Anjaneyasana	Opens chest and stretches groin and thighs

Name of the Pose	Name in Sanskrit	What Are the Benefits?
Marichi's Pose	Marichyasana III	Strengthens and stretches the spine; stretches shoulders; relieves back pain and hip pain; massages abdominal organs
Monkey Pose	Hanumanasana	Intense stretch of thighs, hamstrings, and groin
Mountain Pose	Tadasana	The foundation for all other poses; helps create space in the body; also helps improve posture and controlled breathing
Noose Pose	Pasasana	Promotes a deep stretch of the spine and stimulates abdominal organs
One-Legged King Pigeon Pose I	Eka Pada Rajakapotasana I	A deep backbend that also opens the chest and stretches the hip flexors

Name of the Pose	Name in Sanskrit	What Are the Benefits?
One-Legged King Pigeon Pose II	Eka Pada Rajakapotasana II	Stretches the entire front of the body and also strengthens the muscles of the back
Peacock Pose	Mayurasana	Simultaneously tones abdomen and strengthens wrists, arms, legs, and back
Pendant Pose	Lolasana	Strengthens wrists, tones arm and abdominal muscles, and improves balance
Plank Pose	Kumbhakasana	A forerunner to more challenging arm balances
Plow Pose	Halasana	Stretches the shoulders and spine while also stimulating abdominal organs and the thyroid gland

Name of the Pose	Name in Sanskrit	What Are the Benefits?
Pose Dedicated to the Sage Koundinya I	Eka Pada Koundiyanasana I	Strengthens arms and wrists and also tones abdominal and spinal muscles
Pose Dedicated to the Sage Koundinya II	Eka Pada Koundiyanasana II	Strengthens arms and wrists and also tones abdominal and spinal muscles
Pose Dedicated to the Sage Marichi I	Marichyasana I	Stretches the spine and shoulders and stimulates the abdominal organs, improving digestion
Rabbit Pose	Sasangasana	Stretches back, spine, shoulders, and neck and stimulates thyroid gland
Reclining Big Toe Pose	Supta Padangusthasana	Relieves back pain and stretches hips, hamstrings, and calves

Name of the Pose	Name in Sanskrit	What Are the Benefits?
Reclining Bound Angle Pose	Supta Baddha Konasana	A restorative posture that promotes opening of the hips and groin
Reclining Hero Pose	Supta Virasana	Deeper stretch of the thighs and ankles
Reverse Table Pose	Ardha Purvottanasana	Strengthens core and arm muscles and stretches front side body
Reverse Warrior	Viparita Virabhadrasana	Strengthens the legs and improves spinal flexibility
Revolved Head-to-Knee Pose	Parivrtta Janu Sirsasana	Along with a stretch of the shoulders, spine, and hamstrings is stimulation of abdominal organs and improved digestion

Name of the Pose	Name in Sanskrit	What Are the Benefits?
Revolved Side Angle Pose	Parivrtta Parsvakonasana	Induces a stretch in most of the muscles of the body and also improves stamina
Revolved Triangle Pose	Parivrtta Trikonasana	A counter to Triangle Pose; often a preparation for seated forward bends and twists
Scale Pose	Tolasana	Improves balance in the arms and also strengthens arms and wrists; strengthens abdominal muscles
Scorpion Pose	Vrschikasana	Improves balance, stability, and flexibility and promotes concentration and focus
Seated Forward Bend	Paschimottanasana	Stretches spine, shoulders, and hamstrings and also promotes calming of the mind and relaxation

Name of the Pose	Name in Sanskrit	What Are the Benefits?
Shoulder-Pressing Pose	Bhujapidasana	Builds upper body and arm strength
Side Crane Pose	Parsva Bakasana	Strengthens arms, wrists, and abdomen, lessens back pain, and improves balance
Side Plank Pose, also known as Side-Arm Balance or One-Arm Balance	Vasisthasana	Strengths, arms, wrists, and core
Side-Reclining Leg Lift Pose	Anantasana	Tones the abdominals and stretches the backs of the legs and the sides of the torso
Single Nostril Breath	Surya Bhedana Pranayama	Pressure on the nostrils forces more work on the lungs, promoting a slower, steadier, and fuller breath that helps in recreation of lung tissue and enhances lung capacity

Name of the Pose	Name in Sanskrit	What Are the Benefits?
Skull Shining Breath	Kapalabhati Pranayama	An internal cleansing technique that can be used to cool down the body or can be used as a warm-up for formal pranayama
Sphinx Pose	—	A beginner backbend that strengthens spinal muscles and opens the chest, lungs, shoulders, and abdomen
Staff Pose	Dandasana	Strengthens all major core muscles, improves posture, and increases stamina
Standing Bow Pose	Dandayamana Dhanurasana	Improves balance and strengthens the muscles along the spine
Standing Forward Bend	Uttanasana	Stretches hamstrings and relaxes the mind

Name of the Pose	Name in Sanskrit	What Are the Benefits?
Standing Half Forward Bend, also known as Half Intense Stretch Pose	Ardha Uttanasana	Increases flexibility of the legs and spine muscles
Standing Head to Knee Pose	Dandayamana Janu Sirsasana	Strengthens leg muscles and improves flexibility of the hamstrings
Standing Separate Leg Head to Knee Pose	Dandayamana Bibhaktapada Janushirasana	Tones the core, hips, buttocks, and thighs and also stimulates the thyroid gland
Standing Separate Leg Stretching Pose	Dandayamana Bibhaktapada Paschimotthanasana	Increases flexibility in hamstrings, inner thighs, and spinal muscles and also strengthens arm muscles
Standing Split	Urdhva Prasarita Eka Padasana	Improves balance and induces a deep stretch of the hamstrings and groin muscles

Name of the Pose	Name in Sanskrit	What Are the Benefits?
Supported Headstand	Salamba Sirsasana	Strengthens the entire body while also promoting relaxation in the mind
Supported Shoulderstand	Salamba Sarvangasana	Strengthens legs and bottocks, stretches shoulders and neck, and stimulates thyroid and prostate glands and abdominal organs
Toe Stand	Padangusthasana	Strengthens the knees, relieves rheumatism in the knees, ankles, and feet, and opens the hips
Tree Pose	Vrksasana	Improves balance and tones the muscles of the legs
Triangle Pose	Trikonasana	Strengthens every muscle of the body

Name of the Pose	Name in Sanskrit	What Are the Benefits?
Tortoise Pose	Kurmasana	Opens up hips and shoulders and strengthens muscles of the back
Two Feet behind Head Pose	Dwi Pada Sirsasana	Increases flow of blood throughout the body and is a deep hip opener
Upward Bow or Wheel Pose	Urdhva Dhanurasana	Strengthens arms, legs, and spine and stretches the abdomen
Upward Crouch	Urdhva Paryankasana	Aids in flexibility of the shoulders, neck, lower back, and quadriceps
Upward Facing Dog	Urdhva Mukha Svanasana	Promotes a deep backbend; strengthens arms, wrists, spine, and buttocks; opens the chest and lungs
Upward Facing Two-Foot Staff Pose	Dwi Pada Viparita Dandasana	Stretches the entire front of the body, opens the chest, and strengthens the spine

Name of the Pose	Name in Sanskrit	What Are the Benefits?
Upward Plank Pose	Purvottanasana	Stretches shoulders, chest, and the front of the ankles
Upward Salute (Raised Hands Pose)	Urdhva Hastasana (Tadasana)	Awakens the body through the stretch of all of the muscles of the body
Warrior I Pose	Virabhadrasana I	Strengthens and stretches muscles throughout the body and improves stamina
Warrior II Pose	Virabhadrasana II	Strengthens and stretches muscles throughout the body and improves stamina
Warrior III Pose	Virabhadrasana III	Tones the entire body, especially back and abdominals
Wide-Angle Seated Forward Bend	Upavistha Konasana	Promotes a deep stretch of the insides and backs of legs and strengthens the spine

Name of the Pose	Name in Sanskrit	What Are the Benefits?
Wide-Legged Forward Bend	Prasarita Padottanasana	Promotes a deep stretch of the hamstrings and inner thigh muscles
Wild Thing	Camatkarasana	Opens up the chest, lungs, shoulders, fronts of the legs, and hip flexors
Wind-Removing Pose	Pavanamuktasana	Improves digestion and strengthens hip flexors
Yoga of Sound Breath	Svara Yoga Pranayama	Increases awareness and control of breath
Yogic Sleep Pose	Yoganidrasana	Stretches the deep muscles of the spine and the hip flexors

7

HOT YOGA WISDOM

Suffering is optional.
—Unknown

• • •

To sweat is to pray, to make an offering of your innermost self.
Sweat is holy water, prayer beads, pearls of liquid that release
your past. Sweat is an ancient and universal form of self healing,
whether done in the gym, the sauna, or the sweat lodge . . . The
more you sweat, the more you pray. The more you pray, the closer
you come to ecstasy.
—Gabrielle Roth

• • •

The more we sweat in peace the less we bleed in war.
—VIJAYA LAKSHMI PANDIT

• • •

Yoga maintains youth long. It keeps the body full of vitality,
immune to diseases, even at old, old age. The Yogi never becomes
old.
—BISHNU GHOSH

• • •

Sweat, sweat, sweat! Work and sweat, cry and sweat, pray
and sweat!
—ZORA NEALE HURSTON,
"SWEAT"

• • •

The cure for anything is salt water—sweat, tears, or the sea.
—ISAK DINESEN (KAREN BLIXEN),
AS QUOTED IN *READER'S DIGEST*,
APRIL 1964

• • •

[Regarding a Bikram Yoga session that lasts exactly ninety minutes] Would you rather suffer 90 minutes or 90 years?
—BIKRAM CHOUDHURY

• • •

At first, the idea of doing a 90-minute workout in a 105-degree room sounded like torture. But the sweating is exactly what I became addicted to. My body changed dramatically almost immediately. Within three classes, I noticed less belly fat. My knees and legs are stronger than ever now; my arms have definition for the first time in my life; and my posture is much, much better. I also feel completely energized from all of the deep breathing. I leave class relieved of any anxiety I went in with, and the sweating and detoxifying make my skin feel great.

—REBECCA ROMIJN

• • •

8

GREAT MINDS

I offer you peace. I offer you love. I offer you friendship. I see
your beauty. I hear your need. I feel your feelings. My wisdom
flows from the Highest Source. I salute that Source in you. Let us
work together for unity and love.
—Mahatma Gandhi

• • •

In theory, practice and theory are the same. In practice,
they are not.
—Albert Einstein

• • •

Yoga doesn't take time, it gives time.
—*THE BHAGAVAD GITA*

• • •

When you find peace within yourself, you become the kind of person who can live at peace with others.
—PEACE PILGRIM

• • •

And in the end, it's not the years in your life that count. It's the life in your years.
—ABRAHAM LINCOLN

• • •

If we wish to accomplish dream yoga, it is very important to train in seeing everyday life as a dream.
—KHENCHEN PALDEN SHERAB RINPOCHE

• • •

When you live your life with an appreciation of coincidences and their meanings, you connect with the underlying field of infinite possibilities. This is when the magic begins.
—DEEPAK CHOPRA,
THE SPONTANEOUS FULFILLMENT OF DESIRE:
HARNESSING THE INFINITE POWER OF COINCIDENCE

• • •

The strength of a tree lies in its ability to bend.
—ZEN PROVERB

• • •

It is better to live your own destiny imperfectly than to live an imitation of somebody else's life with perfection.
—*THE BHAGAVAD GITA*

• • •

Yoga believes in transforming the individual before transforming the world.
—SRI SWAMI SATCHIDANANDA

• • •

Knowing only becomes true wisdom when you experience it with your own heart and being. Only the actual experience of this wisdom—gyan—can carry and support you.
—YOGI BHAJAN

• • •

Drop the idea of becoming someone because you are already a masterpiece. You cannot be improved. You have only to come to it to know it, to realize it.
—OSHO, *OSHO ZEN TAROT:*
THE TRANSCENDENTAL GAME OF ZEN

• • •

Your only obligation is in acting, never in results. Don't be the cause of results; and don't have attachment to inaction.
—*THE BHAGAVAD GITA*

• • •

The immature think that knowledge and action are different, but the wise see them as the same.
—*The Bhagavad Gita*

• • •

Who sees all being in his own self, and his own self in all beings, loses all fear.
—*The Isha Upanishad*

• • •

We are not human beings having a spiritual experience, we are spiritual beings having a human experience.
—Pierre Teilhard de Chardin

• • •

Neither in this world or elsewhere is there any happiness in store
for him who always doubts.
—*THE BHAGAVAD GITA*

• • •

The birth and passing away of existences have been heard by me
in detail from Thee, O Lotus-eyed, and also the imperishable
greatness of the divine conscious Soul.
—*THE BHAGAVAD GITA*

• • •

Yoga began with the first person wanting to be healthy and happy
all the time.
—SRI SWAMI SATCHIDANANDA

• • •

Right control of prana (or the life currents) is external, internal or motionless; it is subject to place, time and number and is also protracted or brief.
—PATANJALI,
THE YOGA SUTRAS OF PATANJALI

• • •

The fragrance always remains on the hand that gives the rose.
—MAHATMA GANDHI

• • •

There is nothing noble about being superior to some other man. The nobility is in being superior to your previous self.
—HINDU PROVERB

• • •

When the power of love overcomes the love of power, the world will know peace.
—JIMMY HENDRIX

• • •

The strength of a person does not lie in what he possesses. The strength of a person lies only in that which he is able to give. Only those who have the capacity to reach out into the universe can give something. When the universe is not a part of your mind, your heart is not able to give.
—YOGI BHAJAN

• • •

Nothing can steal happiness, peace away from you: if anyone does make you angry, you are the loser; if someone can allow you to lose peace, you are the loser.
—BIKRAM CHOUDHURY

• • •

We do not need guns and bombs to bring peace, we need love and compassion.
—MOTHER TERESA

● ● ●

Do or do not. There is no try.
—YODA, *STAR WARS:*
THE EMPIRE STRIKES BACK

● ● ●

In this world, there are two persons: the transient and the eternal;
all beings are transient as bodies, but eternal within
the self.
—*THE BHAGAVAD GITA*

• • •

Yoga has brought me to the part of religion I really like
— the positive sides of religion, the parts we all share, rather
than the things that create separation.
—CHRISTY TURLINGTON

• • •

Experience is the only teacher we have.
—SWAMI VIVEKANANDA

• • •

The part can never be well unless the whole is well.
—PLATO

• • •

Leap and the net will appear.
—Zen Proverb

• • •

Understanding and knowledge and freedom from the bewilderment of the Ignorance, forgiveness and truth and self-government and calm of inner control, grief and pleasure, coming into being and destruction, fear and fearlessness, glory and ingloriousness, non-injuring and equality, contentment and austerity and giving, all here in their separate diversities are subjective becomings of existences, and they all proceed from Me.
—*The Bhagavad Gita*

• • •

Always aim at complete harmony of thought and word and deed. Always aim at purifying your thoughts and everything will be well.
—Mahatma Gandhi

• • •

When I despair, I remember that all through history the ways of truth and love have always won. There have been tyrants, and murderers, and for a time they can seem invincible, but in the end they always fall. Think of it—always.
—MAHATMA GANDHI

• • •

Our bodies are our gardens—our wills are our gardeners.
—WILLIAM SHAKESPEARE

• • •

All joy in this world comes from wanting others to be happy, and all suffering in this world comes from wanting only oneself to be happy.
—SHANT IDEVA

• • •

In the midst of movement and chaos, keep stillness inside of you.
—DEEPAK CHOPRA

• • •

The backbone of every ritual is sincere faith.
—SRI SWAMI SATCHIDANANDA

• • •

Yoga practice can make us more and more sensitive to subtler
and subtler sensations in the body. Paying attention to and
staying with finer and finer sensations within the body is one of
the surest ways to steady the wandering mind.
—RAVI RAVINDRA,
*THE WISDOM OF PATANJALI'S YOGA SUTRAS:
A NEW TRANSLATION AND GUIDE BY RAVI RAVINDRA*

• • •

The Universe has given us life and the best thing that we can do
is to love life and to be happy. In Kundalini Yoga we unfurl our
sleeping energy so we can lead a fulfilled, intuitive, and admirable
life in a normal life situation, as a part of this world.
—YOGI BHAJAN

• • •

The five points of *yama*, together with the five points of *niyama*, remind us of the Ten Commandments of the Christian and Jewish faiths, as well as of the ten virtues of Buddhism. In fact, there is no religion without these moral or ethical codes. All spiritual life should be based on these things. They are the foundation stones without which we can never build anything lasting.

—PATANJALI,
THE YOGA SUTRAS OF PATANJALI

● ● ●

Everything is sorrow for the wise.
—PATANJALI,
THE YOGA SUTRAS OF PATANJALI

● ● ●

To the yogi, all experience is seen as one, as a means to help him cultivate devotion. All experiences have equal meaning and value.

—PREM PRAKASH,
THE YOGA OF SPIRITUAL DEVOTION:
A MODERN TRANSLATION OF THE NARADA BHAKTI SUTRAS

● ● ●

On an airplane, you are always told to put on your oxygen mask
first. The same way in life, you need to take care of your health
first. If you are not happy and healthy, you cannot make anyone
else happy and healthy.
—RAJASHREE CHOUDHURY

• • •

If one abstains from food, the objects of sense cease to affect, but
the affection itself of the sense, the rasa, remains; the rasa also
ceases when the Supreme is seen.
—*THE BHAGAVAD GITA*

• • •

Purify yourself and become dust, so that from dust,
flowers can grow.
—RUMI

• • •

Nobility is a virtue that affects every soul
As innocence affects every Heart
Woman has one virtue: to be noble till death
Living nobly is very blessed
Living your truth is happiness

Nobility is a virtue in the presence of God
The greatest virtue that can be expressed
Nobility through everyone whatever they may be
Before the one God equality

A noble woman gives birth to a noble life
Noble children and surroundings be
A noble woman lives nobly and looks noble
Even if she lives in poverty

Unlike a mirror, distorted when it is cracked
Noble habits are a noble life
Don't barter character values for benefits
A noble person does not forget the presence of god

Nobility is manufactured inside
Training to exert self-esteem
To see herself confirms her virtuous face
Selfless living grace through time and space
—ATHANASIOS KARTA SINGH,
"NOBILITY,"
KUNDALINI YOGA:
TECHNIQUES FOR DEVELOPING STRENGTH,
AWARENESS, AND CHARACTER

• • •

And men whose family morals are corrupted, O Janardana, live
for ever in hell. Thus have we heard.
—*THE BHAGAVAD GITA*

• • •

Truth is the same always. Whoever ponders it will get the same
answer. Buddha got it. Patanjali got it. Jesus got it. Mohammed
got it. The answer is the same, but the method of working it out
may vary this way or that.
—PATANJALI,
THE YOGA SUTRAS OF PATANJALI

• • •

It is only when the correct practice is followed for a long time, without interruptions and with a quality of positive attitude and eagerness, that it can succeed.
—PATANJALI,
THE YOGA SUTRAS OF PATANJALI

• • •

It is health that is the real wealth and not pieces of gold and silver.
—MAHATMA GANDHI

• • •

Foster by this the gods and let the gods foster you; fostering each other, you shall attain to the supreme good.
—*THE BHAGAVAD GITA*

• • •

Be soft in your practice. Think of the method as a fine silvery stream, not a raging waterfall.
—Sheng Yen

• • •

Being the richest man in the cemetery doesn't matter to me. Going to bed at night saying we've done something wonderful— that's what matters to me.
—Steve Jobs

• • •

We do not do Kundalini Yoga to become saints; we do it to experience our humanity.
—Yogi Bhajan

• • •

The best way out is always through.
—Robert Frost

• • •

We all wish for world peace, but world peace will never be achieved unless we first establish peace within our own minds.
—Geshe Kelsang Gyatso

• • •

If there is any religion that could respond to the needs of modern science, it would be Buddhism.
—Albert Einstein

• • •

Act without expectation.
—Lao Tzu

• • •

As the soul passes physically through childhood and youth and age, so it passes on to the changing of the body. The self-composed man does not allow himself to be disturbed and blinded by this.
—*The Bhagavad Gita*

• • •

How people treat you is their karma. How you react is yours.
—Wayne Dyer

• • •

Consciousness is one, yet produces the varied forms of the many.
—Patanjali,
The Yoga Sutras of Patanjali

• • •

The entire universe is condensed in the body and the entire body in the Heart. Thus the Heart is the nucleus of the whole universe. This world is not other than the mind, the mind is not other than the Heart; that is the whole truth.
—RAMANA MAHARSHI

• • •

I started doing yoga in my 20s. I did teacher training, that was what I was going to do if acting didn't work out. I started teaching other actors right at the beginning of the yoga craze—people still thought it was a little weird, but a lot of actors I knew were getting into it and didn't want to look foolish in class. So I started teaching them!
—KRISTIN DAVIS

• • •

We are not observers of the universe but its co-creators.
—DEEPAK CHOPRA

• • •

If you see the soul in every living being, you see truly.
—*THE BHAGAVAD GITA*

• • •

The sun shines down, and its image reflects in a thousand different pots filled with water. The reflections are many, but they are each reflecting the same sun. Similarly, when we come to know who we truly are, we will see ourselves in all people.
—AMMA (MATA AMRITANANDAMAYI)

• • •

Watch your thoughts; they become words.
Watch your words; they become actions.
Watch your actions; they become habits.
Watch your habits; they become character.
Watch your character; it becomes your destiny.
—LAO TZU

• • •

The difficulty of those who devote themselves to the search of the unmanifest Brahman is greater; it is a thing to which embodied souls can only arrive by a constant mortification, a suffering of all the repressed members, a stern difficulty and anguish of the nature.
—*THE BHAGAVAD GITA*

• • •

9

REMEMBER TO BREATHE

Breathe through it, and release anything that does not serve you.
—Unknown

• • •

When the breath wanders the mind also is unsteady. But when
the breath is calmed the mind too will be still, and the yogi
achieves long life. Therefore, one should learn to control
the breath.
—*The Hatha Yoga Pradipika*

• • •

I love yoga because not only is it a workout for your body, but also your breathing, which helps release a lot of stress. It really prepares you for the day.
—TIA MOWRY

• • •

Breathing is like a thin thread that can become strong and powerful and be an excellent tool to help us handle situations that otherwise could seem impossible. Breathing is the bridge between our physical and our psychological self and the element that makes it possible for the body, the soul and the mind to become one unity. Breathing is like an engine that makes sure that we live, but conscious breathing can also make us stronger, more resistant, healthier, calmer and harmonic.
—THICH NHAT HANH

• • •

Inhale, and God approaches you. Hold the inhalation, and God remains with you. Exhale, and you approach God. Hold the exhalation, and surrender to God.
—Sri Tirumalai Krishnamacharya

• • •

When you inhale, you are taking the strength from God. When you exhale, it represents the service you are giving to the world.
—B. K. S. Iyengar

• • •

You live through your breath, you are a product of your breath, and the realization of your goals occurs through your breath. In the moment that you are truly united with your breath, the universe streams into you.
—YOGI BHAJAN

• • •

Sometimes it's okay if the only thing you remembered to do today was breathe.
—UNKNOWN

• • •

Without proper breathing, the yoga postures are nothing more than calisthenics.
—RACHEL SCHAEFFER

• • •

When you hold an exhale, prana flows from the upper chakras to the center of the body, to the navel chakra. With a subsequent held exhale, apana rises from the lower chakras to the navel chakra. From this meeting and uniting of both energies in the center of the body comes the so-called *white heat.* It sinks through the sushmana down to the root chakra, where the Kundalini energy awakens. Breath control and power of will allow the Kundalini to rise higher and to come to the higher-seated chakras slowly and continuously. In this manner, lower energies can be dispelled or transformed into higher energies. It is important to cleanse the nadis of blockages and impurities using breath control (pranayama), exercises (asanas), and the engaging of body locks (bandhas) to allow the free flow of Kundalini.

—ATHANASIOS KARTA SINGH,
*KUNDALINI YOGA:
TECHNIQUES FOR DEVELOPING STRENGTH,
AWARENESS, AND CHARACTER*

• • •

Without full awareness of breathing, there can be no development of meditative stability and understanding.
—THICH NHAT HANH

• • •

As a result of pranayama, the covering of the inner light dwindles away.
—PATANJALI,
THE YOGA SUTRAS OF PATANJALI

• • •

Breath is central to yoga because it is central to life . . . and yoga is about life.
—SRI TIRUMALAI KRISHNAMACHARYA

• • •

10

ENLIGHTENMENT

One thing: you have to walk, and create the way by your walking;
you will not find a ready-made path. It is not so cheap, to reach
to the ultimate realization of truth. You will have to create the
path by walking yourself; the path is not ready-made, lying there
and waiting for you. It is just like the sky: the birds fly, but they
don't leave any footprints. You cannot follow them; there are no
footprints left behind.
—Osho

• • •

An enlightened person does not ignore things and does not stick
to things, not even to the truth.
—SHUNRYU SUZUKI

• • •

Knowing others is wisdom, knowing yourself is Enlightenment.
—LAO TZU

• • •

The true value of a human being can be found in the degree to
which he has attained liberation from the self.
—ALBERT EINSTEIN

• • •

It hurts so good and I feel euphoric after . . . yoga people
on a whole are super cool and everyone is there to work on
their own thing.
—HEATHER GRAHAM

• • •

There should be entire rejection of all allurements from all forms
of being, even the celestial, for the recurrence of evil contacts
remains possible.
—PATANJALI,
THE YOGA SUTRAS OF PATANJALI

• • •

A silkworm makes a net of silk and traps herself. Similarly, an individual soul makes a net of plans and desires in the form of the world, and unwittingly imprisons herself. When the traps are broken both fly away.
—BABA HARI DASS

• • •

In Zen Buddhism, the greater your doubt, the greater will be your enlightenment. That is why doubt can be a good thing. If you are too sure, if you always have conviction, then you may be caught in your wrong perception for a long time.
—THICH NHAT HANH

• • •

Enlightenment

Bright but hidden, the Self dwells in the heart. Everything that moves, breathes, opens, and closes lives in the Self—the source of love. Realize the Self hidden in the heart and cut asunder the knot of ignorance here and now.

—*THE UPANISHADS*
AS TRANSLATED BY EKNATH EASWARAN

• • •

I have been practicing yoga for over a decade now, and it is a very important part of my life. It doesn't matter where I am or what I am doing, yoga gives me the opportunity to switch off and focus entirely on my body and my breath. Yoga allows me to meditate and reflect on what's important in my life. It is also great for core strength and maintaining agility.

—Miranda Kerr

• • •

"I shall no longer be instructed by the Yoga Veda or the Aharva Veda, or the ascetics, or any other doctrine whatsoever. I shall learn from myself, be a pupil of myself; I shall get to know myself, the mystery of Siddhartha." He looked around as if he were seeing the world for the first time.

—Hermann Hesse,
Siddhartha

• • •

According to Vedanta, there are only two symptoms of enlightenment, just two indications that a transformation is taking place within you toward a higher consciousness. The first symptom is that you stop worrying. Things don't bother you anymore. You become light-hearted and full of joy. The second symptom is that you encounter more and more meaningful coincidences in your life, more and more synchronicities. And this accelerates to the point where you actually experience the miraculous.
—DEEPAK CHOPRA, *SYNCHRODESTINY:*
HARNESSING THE INFINITE POWER OF COINCIDENCE TO
CREATE MIRACLES

● ● ●

Even if you have not awakened, if you realize that your perceptions and activities are all like dreams and you view them with detachment, not giving rise to grasping and rejecting discrimination, then this is virtually tantamount to awakening from the dream.
—MUSO KOKUSHI

● ● ●

The Blessed Lord said: Thou grievest for those that should not be grieved for. yet speakest words of wisdom. The enlightened man does not mourn either for the living or for the dead.
—*THE BHAGAVAD GITA*

• • •

Many spiritual teachers—in Buddhism, in Islam—have talked about firsthand experience of the world as an important part of the path to wisdom, to enlightenment.
—BELL HOOKS

• • •

Therefore, O mighty-armed, one who has utterly restrained the excitement of the senses by their objects, his intelligence sits firmly founded in calm self-knowledge.
—*THE BHAGAVAD GITA*

• • •

As in music, when we hear the crescendo building, suddenly if
the music stops, we begin to hear the silence as part of the music.
—CHÖGYAM TRUNGPA,
CUTTING THROUGH SPIRITUAL MATERIALISM

• • •

When the means to yoga have been steadily practised, and when
impurity has been overcome, enlightenment takes place, leading
up to full illumination.
—PATANJALI,
THE YOGA SUTRAS OF PATANJALI

• • •

Enlightenment must come little by little—otherwise it
would overwhelm.
—IDRIES SHAH

• • •

Enlightenment is permanent because we have not produced it.
We have merely discovered it.
—CHÖGYAM TRUNGPA

• • •

When thy intelligence which is bewildered by the Sruti, shall stand unmoving and stable in Samadhi, then shalt thou attain to Yoga.
—*The Bhagavad Gita*

• • •

As unobtainable, as you have heard, that Enlightenment is, it is in fact within your reach, already waiting within the palm of your hand. Not much stands in your way. Nothing that you could not move in one day.
—Dave Oshana

• • •

Those whose consciousness is unified abandon all attachment to the results of action and attain supreme peace. But those whose desires are fragmented, who are selfishly attached to the results of their work, are bound in everything they do.
—*The Bhagavad Gita*

• • •

Trying to find a buddha or enlightenment is like trying to grab space.
—Bodhidharma

• • •

In the case of the man who has achieved yoga (or union) the objective universe has ceased to be. Yet it existeth still for those who are not yet free.
—PATANJALI,
THE YOGA SUTRAS OF PATANJALI

• • •

Enlightenment is always there. Small enlightenment will bring great enlightenment. If you breathe in and are aware that you are alive—that you can touch the miracle of being alive—then that is a kind of enlightenment.
—THICH NHAT HANH

• • •

Not thinking about anything is Zen. Once you know this, walking, sitting, or lying down, everything you do is Zen.
—BODHIDHARMA,
THE ZEN TEACHING OF BODHIDHARMA

• • •

One does not become enlightened by imagining figures of light, but by making the darkness conscious.
—CARL JUNG

• • •

Who abandons all desires and lives and acts free from longing,
who has no "I" or "mine" (who has extinguished his individual
ego in the One and lives in that unity), he attains to the
great peace.
—*THE BHAGAVAD GITA*

• • •

If I could define enlightenment briefly I would say it is the quiet
acceptance of what is.
—WAYNE DYER

• • •

Everyone has a spirit that can be refined, a body that can be
trained in some manner, a suitable path to follow. You are here to
realize your inner divinity and manifest your innate
enlightenment.
—MORIHEI UESHIBA

• • •

When a poet digs himself into a hole, he doesn't climb out. He digs deeper, enjoys the scenery, and comes out the other side enlightened.
—CRISS JAMI,
VENUS IN ARMS

• • •

Allow the river of the mind
to flow freely,
without conceptual constraint,
through the open landscape of awareness,
and the gold of realization
will wash up on its own.
—GEORG FEUERSTEIN,
"RIVER'S GOLD,"
TRANSPARENT LEAVES FROM THE TREE OF LIFE

• • •

The obstacles to soul cognition are bodily disability, mental inertia, wrong questioning, carelessness, laziness, lack of dispassion, erroneous perception, inability to achieve concentration, failure to hold the meditative attitude when achieved.
—Patanjali,
The Yoga Sutras of Patanjali

• • •

I didn't have to go all the way to India for spiritual enlightenment. The blue-collar spirituality of everyday life was right in front of me, it was in every nook and cranny if I wanted to seek it, but I had chosen to ignore it.
—Anthony Kiedis,
Scar Tissue

• • •

An enlightened man had but one duty - to seek the way to himself, to reach inner certainty, to grope his way forward, no matter where it led.
—Hermann Hesse,
Demian

• • •

And as long as you're subject to birth and death, you'll never attain enlightenment.
—Bodhidharma

• • •

Enlightenment is not something you achieve. It is the absence of something. All your life you have been going forward after something, pursuing some goal. Enlightenment is dropping all that.
—CHARLOTTE J. BECK

• • •

Everybody wants to get enlightened but nobody wants to change.
—ANDREW COHEN

• • •

Earth and sky, woods and fields, lakes and rivers, the mountain and the sea, are excellent schoolmasters, and teach some of us more than we can ever learn from books.
—JOHN LUBBOCK

• • •

I don't believe that human beings can achieve ultimate
enlightenment, because humans have flaws.
—TIGER WOODS

• • •

Don't think you can attain total awareness and whole
enlightenment without proper discipline and practice. This is
egomania. Appropriate rituals channel your emotions and life
energy toward the light. Without the discipline to practice them,
you will tumble constantly backward into darkness.
—LAO TZU

• • •

Not till your thoughts cease all their branching here and there,
not till you abandon all thoughts of seeking for something, not
till your mind is motionless as wood or stone, will you be on the
right road to the Gate.
—HUANG PO,
*THE ZEN TEACHING OF HUANG PO:
ON THE TRANSMISSION OF MIND*

• • •

Despair is the result of each earnest attempt to go through life with virtue, justice and understanding, and to fulfill their requirements. Children live on one side of despair, the awakened on the other side.
—HERMANN HESSE,
THE JOURNEY TO THE EAST

• • •

Enlightenment will be now the beginning, not the end. Beginning of a non-ending process in all dimensions of richness.
—OSHO

• • •

Once again, we are reminded that awakening, or enlightenment is not the property of Buddhism, any more than Truth is the property of Christianity. Neither the Buddha nor the Christ belongs exclusively to the communities that were founded in their names. They belong to all people of goodwill, all who are attentive to the secret which lives in the depths of their breath and their consciousness.
—JEAN-YVES LELOUP,
COMPASSION AND MEDITATION:
THE SPIRITUAL DYNAMIC BETWEEN BUDDHISM AND
CHRISTIANITY

• • •

The Stone of Guilt in the River of the Mind, the block in the flow of intelligence.
—PARAMAHAMSA NITHYANANDA,
LIVING ENLIGHTENED

• • •

It [enlightenment] has not come to you by means of teaching! And—thus is my thought, oh exalted one,—nobody will obtain salvation by means of teachings!
—SIDDHARTHA TO BUDDHA,
SIDDHARTHA BY HERMANN HESSE

• • •

A person must earn enlightenment, Eragon. It is not handed down to you by others, regardless of how revered they be.
—CHRISTOPHER PAOLINI,
BRISINGR

• • •

11

LIGHTEN UP

Blessed are the flexible, for they shall not be bent out of shape.
—Unknown

• • •

When asked what gift he wanted for his birthday, the yogi
replied, "I wish no gifts, only presence."
—Unknown

• • •

The yoga mat is a good place to turn when talk therapy and antidepressants aren't enough.
—AMY WEINTRAUB

• • •

If God had intended us to do yoga, he would have put our heads behind our knees.
—ROD STEWART

• • •

If everyone practiced yoga, pharmacies would have to close.
—B. K. S. IYENGAR

• • •

Don't just do something—sit there!
—UNKNOWN

• • •

I was in yoga the other day. I was in full lotus position. My chakras were all aligned. My mind is cleared of all clatter, and I'm looking out of my third eye and everything that I'm supposed to be doing. It's amazing what comes up when you sit in that silence. "Mama keeps whites bright like the sunlight; Mama's got the magic of Clorox Two."
—ELLEN DEGENERES

• • •

My Karma ran over your Dogma.
—Unknown

• • •

HELLO! Look at me. HELLO! I am so ZEN. This is BLOOD. This is NOTHING. Hello. Everything is nothing, and it's so cool to be ENLIGHTENED. Like me.
—Chuck Palahniuk,
Fight Club

• • •

Let's face it, I only practice yoga because the classes are always packed with beautiful women.
—Adam Levine

• • •

The road to enlightenment is long and difficult, and you should try not to forget snacks and magazines.
—Anne Lamott,
*Traveling Mercies:
Some Thoughts on Faith*

• • •

If you begin to feel faint or dizzy, stop breathing and relax!
—Unknown (when teaching Kapalabhati breathing)

• • •

Remember, it is more important for a smile to spread over your shin than it is to get your chin closer to your shin.
—Stuart Rice

• • •

If you're not barefoot, then you're overdressed.
—Unknown

• • •

Without love, without humor, yoga is just a lot of hard work.
—Steve Ross

• • •

A lot of people question how yoga and their own spiritual beliefs can come together. Yoga actually pre-dates religion.
—Christy Turlington

• • •

To Do Today, 1/17/08
1. Sit and think
2. Reach enlightenment
3. Feed the cats
—JAROD KINTZ,
I SHOULD HAVE RENAMED THIS

• • •

A young woman who was worried about her habit of biting her fingernails down to the quick was advised by a friend to take up yoga. She did, and soon her fingernails were growing normally. Her friend asked her if yoga had totally cured her nervousness. "No," she replied, "but now I can reach my toe-nails so I bite them instead."
—UNKNOWN

• • •

Religions have always stressed that compassion is not only central to religious life, it is the key to enlightenment and is the true test of spirituality. But there have always been those who'd rather put easier goals, like doctrine conformity, in place.
—KAREN ARMSTRONG

• • •

Maybe the Truth of the Meaning of Life, Ancient and Arcane Knowledge of the Great Unknowable Universe is handed down only to persons presenting with the correct brand-name footwear. If you turn up wearing Shoe City knock-offs, you don't get to pass Go and collect Infinite Enlightenment.
—TRACY ENGELBRECHT,
THE GIRL WHO COULDN'T SAY NO

• • •

I think it would be a good idea.
—MAHATMA GANDHI
(WHEN ASKED WHAT HE THOUGHT ABOUT WESTERN
CIVILIZATION)

• • •

Change is inevitable, except from vending machines.
—UNKNOWN

• • •

When you laugh you change, when you change, the whole
world changes.
—DR. MADAN KATARIA,
FOUNDER OF LAUGHTER YOGA

• • •

They say that god is everywhere, and yet we always think of Him
as somewhat of a recluse.
—EMILY DICKINSON

• • •

Meditation and water are wedded forever.
—HERMAN MELVILLE

• • •

You're only one yoga pose away from a good mood.
—UNKNOWN

• • •

If we remove ourselves from the world, we are pretending that we can follow our own individual enlightenment and let the rest of the world go to hell, so to speak.
—SATISH KUMAR

• • •

The best vitamin to be a happy person is B1.
—UNKNOWN

• • •

It's not that I'm afraid to die. I just don't want to be there when it happens.
—WOODY ALLEN

• • •

Even after enlightenment, you still have to do the laundry.
—UNKNOWN

• • •

I would say any behavior that is not the status quo is interpreted as insanity, when, in fact, it might actually be enlightenment. Insanity is sorta in the eye of the beholder.
—CHUCK PALAHNIUK

• • •

12

WHAT'S IN A POSE?

The posture assumed must be steady and easy.
—Patanjali,
The Yoga Sutras of Patanjali

• • •

Sun salutations can energize and warm you, even on the darkest,
coldest winter day.
—Carol Krucoff

• • •

Corpse Pose restores life. Dead parts of your being falling away,
the ghosts are released.
—The Quote Garden

• • •

Perfection in asana is achieved when the effort to perform it
becomes effortless and the infinite being within is reached.
—Patanjali

• • •

Warrior pose battles inner weakness and wins focus. You see that
there is no war within you. You're on your own side, and you are
your own strength.
—Terri Guillemets

• • •

Chair pose is a defiance of spirit, showing how high you can
reach even when you're forced down.
—Terri Guillemets

• • •

The yoga pose that you avoid the most you need the most.
—Unknown

• • •

Concentrating on poses clears the mind, while focusing on the breath helps the body shift out of fight-or-flight mode.
—Melanie Haiken

• • •

Asana (posture) should be steady and comfortable.
—Patanjali,
The Yoga Sutras of Patanjali

• • •

Stirum sukham asanam. Seated posture should be steady and comfortable.
—Patanjali,
The Yoga Sutras of Patanjali

• • •

The pose begins when you want to leave it.

—Unknown

• • •

In Kundalini yoga, there is a multitude of seated asanas. There are many variations to choose from based on physical condition and skill level.

—Athanasios Karta Singh,
Kundalini Yoga:
Techniques for Developing Strength,
Awareness, and Character

• • •

Asanas bring perfection in body, beauty in form, grace, strength, compactness, and the harness and brilliance of a diamond.
—PATANJALI,
THE YOGA SUTRAS OF PATANJALI

• • •

Remember, it doesn't matter how deep into a posture you go—what does matter is who you are when you get there.
—MAX STROM

• • •

If I'm losing balance in a pose, I stretch higher and God reaches down to steady me. It works every time, and not just in yoga.
—TERRI GUILLEMETS

• • •

Asanas attune the body to meditation, just as a guitar is tuned before a performance.
—Unknown

• • •

When right posture (asana) has been attained there follows right control of prana and proper inspiration and expiration of the breath.
—Patanjali,
The Yoga Sutras of Patanjali

• • •

The feeling in the spiritual heart must be, "I am not separate from asana, asana is not separate from me, I am asana and asana is me."
—B. K. S. Iyengar

• • •

13

YOGA IS A JOURNEY

Yoga is not about self-improvement, it's about self-acceptance.
—Gurmukh Kaur Khalsa

• • •

Starting out in a beginner class and really understanding the
fundamentals of yoga is really important.
—Mariel Hemingway

• • •

If you do not change direction, you may end up where
you are heading.
—Lao Tzu

• • •

It's been my experience that the longer I do yoga, the more I want to know, the more I am able to understand, and the less judgmental I am.
—ALI MACGRAW

• • •

And you? When will you begin that long journey into yourself?
—RUMI

• • •

Many paths are possible; whichever path is sincerely traveled leads to inner peace.
—*THE BHAGAVAD GITA*

• • •

You are allowed to take to heart the things that resonate with you and leave the rest.
—*THE YOGA JOURNAL*

• • •

It is better to travel well than to arrive.
—GAUTAMA BUDDHA

• • •

The journey of 1,000 miles begins with one step.
—LAO TZU

• • •

Constant practice alone is the secret of success.
—*THE HATHA YOGA PRADIPIKA*

• • •

Strength and growth come only through continuous effort
and struggle.
—NAPOLEON HILL

• • •

When the sage climbs the heights of yoga, he follows the path
of work; but when he reaches the heights of yoga, he is in the
land of peace.
—*THE BHAGAVAD GITA*

• • •

First month paining, second month tired, third month flying.
—Sharath Jois

• • •

There are no shortcuts to growth, but there are moments of rapid acceleration.
—Unknown

• • •

When you find your path, you must not be afraid. You need to have sufficient courage to make mistakes. Disappointment, defeat, and despair are the tools God uses to show us the way.
—Paulo Coelho, *Brida*

• • •

I had discovered something; there was a pleasure in becoming something new. You could will yourself into a fresh shape. Now all I had to do was figure out how to do it out there, in my life.
—Claire Dederer,
Poser:
My Life in Twenty-Three Yoga Poses

• • •

At various points in our lives, or on a quest, and for reasons that often remain obscure, we are driven to make decisions which prove with hindsight to be loaded with meaning.
—PATANJALI,
THE YOGA SUTRAS OF PATANJALI

● ● ●

Every time you are tempted to react in the same old way, ask if you want to be a prisoner of the past, or a pioneer of the future.
—DEEPAK CHOPRA

● ● ●

We are not going in circles, we are going upwards. The path is a spiral; we have already climbed many steps.
—HERMANN HESSE

● ● ●

Any belief, whatever it is, is counterproductive in the context of
the practice of yoga. One holds a belief instead of knowing. For
example, you wouldn't say you believe in your right ear, since you
know your ear, no belief is required. Believing always excludes
knowing. When jnana (supreme knowledge) comes through
the practice of yoga, you will know. Do not be satisfied with
believing.
—GREGOR MAEHLE

• • •

Yoga is not about touching your toes. It's about what you learn on
the way down.
—UNKNOWN

• • •

You are never too old to set another goal or to dream
a new dream.
—C. S. LEWIS

• • •

One becomes firmly established in practice only after attending
to it for a long time, without interruption and with an attitude
of devotion.
—PATANJALI,
THE YOGA SUTRAS OF PATANJALI

• • •

All great changes are preceded by chaos.
—DEEPAK CHOPRA

• • •

People take different roads seeking fulfillment and happiness. Just
because they're not on your road does not mean they
are lost.
—DALAI LAMA

• • •

14

MEDITATION

Meditation is such a more substantial reality than what we
normally take to be reality.
—RICHARD GERE

• • •

Sleep is the best meditation.
—DALAI LAMA

• • •

Meditation is a vital element of KUNDALINI YOGA. The goal of meditation is to open and to come to know the mind through attentiveness and concentration.
—ATHANASIOS KARTA SINGH,
KUNDALINI YOGA:
TECHNIQUES FOR DEVELOPING STRENGTH,
AWARENESS, AND CHARACTER

• • •

Peace (steadiness of the chitta) can be reached through meditation on the knowledge which dreams give.
—PATANJALI,
THE YOGA SUTRAS OF PATANJALI

• • •

When meditation is mastered, the mind is unwavering like the flame of a lamp in a windless place.
—*THE BHAGAVAD GITA*

• • •

Reading makes a full man, meditation a profound man,
discourse a clear man.
—Benjamin Franklin

• • •

Better indeed is knowledge than mechanical practice. Better
than knowledge is meditation. But better still is surrender of
attachment to results, because there follows immediate peace.
—*The Bhagavad Gita*

• • •

The gift of learning to meditate is the greatest gift you can give
yourself in this lifetime.
—Sogyal Rinpoche

• • •

My workout is my meditation.
—KYLE MACLACHLAN

• • •

Through meditation, one-pointedly fixed upon the sun, will come a consciousness (or knowledge) of the seven worlds.
—PATANJALI,
THE YOGA SUTRAS OF PATANJALI

• • •

Meditation brings wisdom; lack of meditation leaves ignorance. Know well what leads you forward and what holds you back, and choose the path that leads to wisdom.
—Gautama Buddha

• • •

The affairs of the world will go on forever. Do not delay the practice of meditation.
—Jetsun Milarepa

• • •

Through meditation and by giving full attention to one thing at a time, we can learn to direct attention where we choose.
—EKNATH EASWARAN

• • •

Meditation is a duty to the self. In the moment in which you become aware of your own self, you become beautiful. Because, in the moment in which you concentrate on the self, your frequency changes and the universe around you changes in the exact same way. That is a funny law.
—YOGI BHAJAN

• • •

One-pointed meditation upon the five forms which every element takes, produces mastery over every element. These five forms are the gross nature, the elemental form, the quality, the pervasiveness and the basic purpose.
—PATANJALI,
THE YOGA SUTRAS OF PATANJALI

• • •

True meditation is about being fully present with everything that is—including discomfort and challenges. It is not an escape from life.
—CRAIG HAMILTON

• • •

[T]he period between four and six in the morning is called the *Brahmamuhurta*, the Brahmic time, or divine period, and is a very sacred time to meditate.
—PATANJALI,
THE YOGA SUTRAS OF PATANJALI

• • •

Silence is not silent. Silence speaks. It speaks most eloquently. Silence is not still. Silence leads. It leads most perfectly.
—SRI CHINMOY

• • •

Every soul innately yearns for stillness, for a space, a garden where we can till, sow, reap, and rest, and by doing so come to a deeper sense of self and our place in the universe. Silence is not an absence but a presence. Not an emptiness but repletion. A filling up.
—ANNE D. LECLAIRE,
LISTENING BELOW THE NOISE:
A MEDITATION ON THE PRACTICE OF SILENCE

• • •

Mastery over the senses is brought about through concentrated meditation upon their nature, peculiar attributes, egoism, pervasiveness and useful purpose.
—PATANJALI,
THE YOGA SUTRAS OF PATANJALI

• • •

Don't think that only when you close your eyes, you are meditating. Anything that you do with total attention is meditation.
—SRI SWAMI SATCHIDANANDA

• • •

The practice of drishti yoga calls for utmost devoutness and tenacity of purpose. The practitioner who assiduously and patiently practices this meditation will discover that the fickleness or unsteadiness of their concentration gradually ceases and their mind becomes tranquil. It is thus that they shall, with the piercing thrust of their focused gaze, be able to break open the 'tila dwara' (Third Eye).
—SWAMI ACHYUTANAND BABA

• • •

INDEX